EssexWorks.
For a better quality of life

D0714687

STORYTELLER:
CHRISTIAN STORIES

Evans Brothers Limited
2a Portman Mansions
Chiltern Street
London W1U 6NR

First published in paperback in 2007

British Library Cataloguing Data
Ganeri, Anita
   Christian stories, – (Storyteller)
   1. Christianity – Juvenile literature
   I.Title Il.Phillips, Rachel
   230

ISBN 0 237 52752 9
13-digit ISBN 978 0 237 52752 5

Editor: Victoria Brooker
Series Editor: Su Swallow
Designer: Simon Borrough
Illustrations: Rachael Phillips, Allied Artists
Production: Jenny Mulvanny
Consultant: Reverend Graham Owen
text copyright © Anita Ganeri 2001
© in the illustrations Evans Brothers
Limited 2001

Printed in China by WKT Co.Ltd

Acknowledgements
The author and publishers would like to
thank the following for permission to
reproduce copyright material: page 6 Trip/H
Rogers, page 10 Trip/P Rauter, page 13
N Hall/Shout/Robert Harding Picture
Library, page 17 Trip/J Stanley, page 20
Trip/J Wakelin, page 23 (left) Trip/H Rogers
(right) Pal Hermansen/Tony Stone Images,
page 25 Trip/M Fairman, page 28 Trip/
M Jelliffe.

VISIT OUR WEBSITE
Evans
www.evansbooks.co.uk

STORYTELLER: CHRISTIAN STORIES

Anita Ganeri

Illustrations by Rachael Phillips

Evans Brothers Limited

Introduction

Christian Stories

In each of the world's six main religions – Hinduism, Judaism, Buddhism, Christianity, Islam and Sikhism – stories play a very important part. They have been used for many hundreds of years to teach people about their faith in a way which makes difficult messages easier to understand. Many stories tell of episodes in the lives of religious teachers, leaders, gods and goddesses. Others explain mysterious events such as how the world was created or what happens when we die. Many have a strong moral or lesson to teach.

The collection of stories you can read in this book comes from the Christian religion. Christianity began in the Middle East about 2000 years ago. Christians follow the teachings of Jesus. They believe that Jesus was the son of God who came to Earth to teach people more about God.

The stories of Jesus's life and teaching are told in the New Testament of the Bible, the Christian holy book. The first four books of the New Testament are called the Gospels and these were written by four early Christians, Matthew, Mark, Luke and John.

Contents

The Birth of Jesus

Long, long ago, in the town of Nazareth in Galilee, there lived a young woman called Mary. She was engaged to be married to the local carpenter, Joseph. One day, when Mary was busy with her daily chores, the room was filled with light and the angel Gabriel appeared before her. Mary felt very afraid.

"Don't be frightened, Mary," the angel said. "This is a happy day. For God has chosen you to have a baby. A very special baby who will become the saviour of the world. And his name will be Jesus."

"I will do as God wishes," Mary said, bowing her head. When she looked up, the angel had gone. Later he visited Joseph to bless his marriage to Mary.

Soon afterwards, Mary and Joseph were married. They settled down in Nazareth to look forward to the baby's birth. But their settled life did not last for long. Some months later, the emperor ordered everyone to return to the town of their birth to be counted and taxed. Joseph was born in Bethlehem, a town far away, and he and Mary had to go back there.

It was a long and tiring journey. Mary rode on a donkey while Joseph walked in front. At night they slept by the roadside. And when at last they reached Bethlehem, the town was crowded with travellers like them. Joseph knew that the baby would

Did you know?

Each year, Christians all over the world celebrate Jesus's birth with church services, gifts, cards and special food. No one knows exactly when Jesus was born. The first Christians chose 25 December because this was the date of another ancient winter festival. Some Christians celebrate Christmas Day on 6 January, the day on which they remember the wise men's visit to Jesus.

soon be born and he anxiously went from door to door, looking for somewhere for them to stay. But everywhere was full. A kindly innkeeper took pity on them.

"I don't have a room to spare," he said, "But you're welcome to sleep in my stable." And, later that night, in the snug little stable, Mary had her baby. She called him Jesus, as the angel had told her. She wrapped him up warmly and laid him in a manger on a bed of soft hay. The manger

was where the animals usually had their food but there was nowhere else for the baby to sleep.

Meanwhile, on a hillside outside the town, a group of shepherds were watching over their sheep. It was late at night and some of the shepherds were dozing off to sleep. Suddenly the sky was filled with dazzling light. The shepherds were terrified and dared not look. When they finally opened their eyes and looked, an angel stood before them.

"I bring you wonderful news," the angel said. "Today a baby has been born in Bethlehem who will be the saviour of the world. Go quickly and visit him. You will find him lying in a manger."

Then the sky was filled with angels, singing:

"Glory to God in the highest,
And on Earth peace,
Good will to all people."

As soon as the angels had gone, the shepherds hurried to Bethlehem to see Jesus. They found him in the stable, as the angel had promised, and knelt down quietly to worship him. Then they returned to their fields. On the way, they told everyone they met about the amazing things they had seen and heard.

News of Jesus's birth spread far and wide throughout the country. A group of wise men travelled from the east to Jerusalem to look for the baby. A few nights earlier, they had

Did you know?

Angels play an important part in Christian stories. They are believed to be heavenly beings who carry messages and prayers between Heaven and Earth. In the Bible, the archangel Gabriel brings messages from God to people on Earth. It is he who announces the birth of Jesus. Angels are often pictured as beautiful, shining beings, flying on wings and with haloes around their heads. Their beauty is a sign of God's glory.

seen a bright star in the sky, a sign that a new king had been born, as the ancient scriptures had said. Now they wanted to worship him for themselves. But when King Herod, the ruler of Jerusalem, heard their story, he was furious. He did not want a rival for his power. So he summoned the wise men to see him.

"Once you have found the baby, return to me," he told them. "So that I can worship him too."

But wicked Herod did not want to worship Jesus. He was really plotting to kill him.

The three wise men left Jerusalem and

followed the star to Bethlehem. There they found Mary, Joseph and the baby Jesus. With great joy, they knelt down and worshipped him, and gave him their gifts of precious gold, frankincense and myrrh. Gifts that were fit for a king. That night, each of them had the same dream, warning them not to return to Jerusalem but to go home by a different route. Then Herod would not find them.

Soon after the wise men left, Joseph saw an angel in his dreams.

"Take Mary and Jesus and go to Egypt," the angel said. "Go quickly, there is no time to lose. Herod is looking for the baby and if he finds him, he will surely kill him."

Joseph woke Mary, and they crept out of the house, taking Jesus with them. Their journey to Egypt took many days but at last they reached safety. They stayed there until an angel visited Joseph again, this time with good news. Herod was dead, and, at last, Mary, Joseph and Jesus were able to go home to Nazareth.

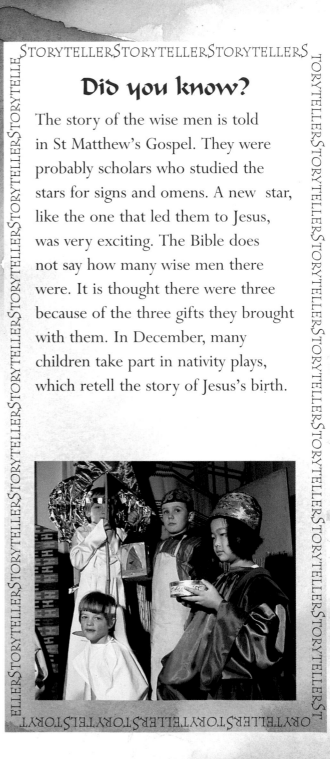

Did you know?

The story of the wise men is told in St Matthew's Gospel. They were probably scholars who studied the stars for signs and omens. A new star, like the one that led them to Jesus, was very exciting. The Bible does not say how many wise men there were. It is thought there were three because of the three gifts they brought with them. In December, many children take part in nativity plays, which retell the story of Jesus's birth.

Jesus is Baptised

At the time Jesus was growing up, his cousin, John the Baptist, was already busy teaching people about God. He lived a very hard and simple life, wandering from place to place, preaching and teaching to all those who would listen. Instead of fine cloth, John wore a robe of rough camel hair, tied with a leather belt. Instead of fine food, all he had to eat were locusts and wild honey. People came from far and wide to hear John speak.

"If you are truly sorry for your sins and wrong-doings," he told them, "you will reach God's kingdom in Heaven."

"But how can we live better lives?" they asked him.

"Firstly, you must be kind to others," John said. "Share whatever you have. If you have two coats, give one away. And if you have plenty of food, give some to the hungry. Try not to hurt anyone or tell lies about them."

People listened eagerly to John's words and many came forward to be baptised. In this way they could show that they were truly willing to change their ways and to live as God wanted. John baptised them in the River Jordan. He also told them that a great teacher was coming who would be much more important than he was.

One day, Jesus came to hear John speak and he asked John to baptise him. John was surprised and did not know what to do. He knew that Jesus was the great teacher he had spoken of.

"It is you who should baptise me," he said, softly. "Not I who should baptise you."

But Jesus walked into the river, and John baptised him there. Just at that moment, it was as though the heavens opened and the Holy Spirit came down to Jesus like a dove descending from the sky. They heard God's voice saying:

"You are my own dear son. I am pleased with you."

Jesus was almost thirty years old. After his baptism, he was ready for the special work which God had given him to do.

Did you know?

Most Christians today are baptised at a ceremony in a church. During Baptism people are accepted into the Christian faith. They are sprinkled with or dipped in water as a symbol of washing away their sins. Then the sign of the cross is made on their forehead to show that they have promised to follow Jesus. Another name for Baptism is Christening. Baptism can take place at any stage in life. Some people are baptised as babies. Others wait until they are adults.

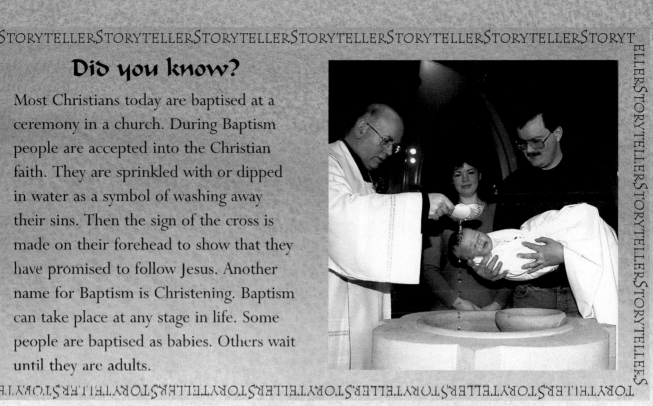

Did you know?

John the Baptist was the son of Zechariah, a priest, and his wife, Elizabeth who was the cousin of Mary, Jesus's mother. The Bible tells how the angel Gabriel appeared to Zechariah to tell him that he would have a son. Zechariah did not believe him. He thought that he and his wife were too old to have children. Because Zechariah doubted him, Gabriel struck him dumb but his voice came back when John was born, just as the angel had said.

Fishers of People

One day, as Jesus was walking by the Sea of Galilee, he saw some fishing boats pulled up on the shore. One of the boats belonged to two brothers, Simon Peter and Andrew. Jesus stopped to talk to the fishermen. He stepped on to Simon's boat and asked him to row a little way out into the lake. Then Jesus sat down in the boat and began to teach the crowds who had started to gather on the shore.

When he had finished speaking and the people had begun to go home, Jesus said to the brothers:

"Let's sail a little further out, into deeper water, then cast your nets again."

"It won't do any good," Simon Peter replied. "We've been out all night and we

The brothers could not believe their eyes. It was the biggest catch they had ever seen. They fell on their knees in front of Jesus. They did not know what else to do.

"Come and follow me," Jesus told them. "And I will make you into fishers of people. You will be my disciples and help me spread God's message." And so the brothers left their nets and their boats behind them, to follow Jesus on the greatest adventure of their lives.

haven't caught a single fish."

Nevertheless, the brothers did as Jesus asked and threw their fishing nets overboard. To their astonishment, the nets were soon filled with so many fish that one net broke and the other was too heavy to pull into the boat. The brothers had to call another boat over, and together they hauled the bulging nets on board.

Did you know?

A disciple is a follower of a teacher or leader. In the Bible, Jesus chose 12 men as his special disciples to help him to carry out his work. Their names were Simon Peter, Andrew, James, John, Philip, Bartholomew, Thomas, Matthew, James, Thaddeus, Simon and Judas. They were among Jesus's closest friends.

Did you know?

Fishing was a very important industry around the Sea of Galilee. At night, the fishermen set sail in their small, wooden boats to cast their nets for fish. They returned to shore next morning. The lake is often hit by violent storms, like the one in the story. Cold air from the nearby mountains sweeps down and whips up the water into huge waves. The storms strike very suddenly but pass just as quickly as they blow up.

It was a calm, warm evening by the Sea of Galilee. The lake was peaceful and still as Jesus and his disciples got into a boat to cross to the other side. Jesus was very tired. He had spent the day teaching the crowds on the lake shore and had not had a minute to himself. As soon as he got into the boat, he lay down and fell fast asleep.

Suddenly, with no warning at all, a strong, gusty wind began to blow. The wind whipped the water into angry waves and tossed the boat from side to side. The disciples struggled to keep going. To their horror, the storm got worse. Huge waves lashed over the sides of the boat and soon it began to fill with water.

Many of the disciples were hardy fishermen. They were used to storms and had seen many of them before. But they had never known anything as bad as this. Now they were frightened for their lives, sure that they were going to drown. They went to where Jesus lay sleeping and shook him to wake him up.

"Master," they cried. "Wake up, wake up! We're sinking. Whatever shall we do?"

Jesus got up and stood on the deck.

"Be still!" he commanded the wind.

And the wind was still.

"Be still!" he commanded the water.

And the water was still.

Then Jesus turned to his disciples. "Where is your faith?" he asked them. "If you believe in God, you need not be afraid of anything."

The Good Samaritan

This is the story Jesus told of a Good Samaritan who stopped to help a stranger and became an example for others to follow. One day, a man was walking along the road from Jerusalem to the town of Jericho. The road, as usual, was almost deserted. Now and again, a traveller or two passed by on a donkey but for most of the time, the man was on his own. This was a dangerous road, famous for bandits and robbers. But he had walked this way many times before and never had any trouble.

This time the man was not so lucky. A gang of robbers had been watching him, from their hiding place among the roadside bushes. When he got nearer, they jumped out and attacked him. They stole his clothes and all his belongings, and left him for dead. Then they ran away.

Some time later, a traveller passed by on his way to Jerusalem. But when he saw the injured man, he looked away and quickly crossed the road. After all, he thought, it wasn't any of his business. He didn't want to get involved. Then another man came down the road. Like the first man, he could have helped the traveller. But he too hurried by without even stopping.

Then a third man, a Samaritan, came by. When he saw the man and how much he was suffering, he felt very sad. At once, he stopped and got off his donkey. Gently, he cleaned the man's wounds with oil and wine, and bound them up with strips of cloth, torn from his own clothes. Then he put the man on the back of his donkey and led him to a nearby inn where he could take care of him.

Next day, the Samaritan had to carry on with his journey. He had urgent business in the next town. But before he left, he gave the innkeeper some money.

"Look after my friend," he told the innkeeper, "and don't let him leave until he is better. If you need more money, spend what you must, and I will repay you when I come back again."

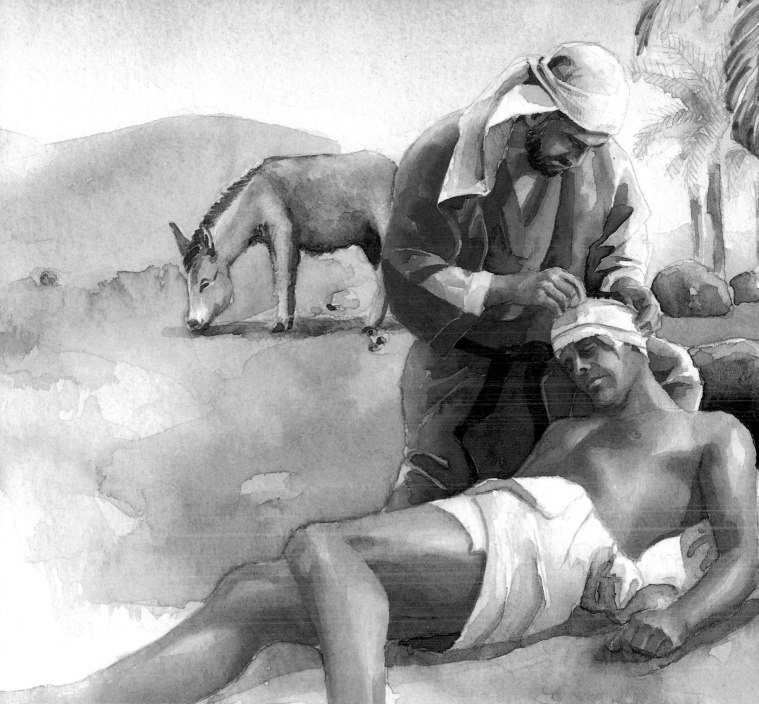

Did you know?

The Samaritan came from the city of Samaria in central Palestine. In Jesus's time, the Jews and Samaritans did not get along. The Jews treated Samaritans as outsiders. The other travellers in the story were important holy men who should have known better. Yet it was a Samaritan who stopped to help the injured man. Jesus used this story to teach the importance of being kind and caring to everyone, no matter who they are or where they come from.

The Sower and the Seed

Jesus often taught by the Sea of Galilee. One day, such a large crowd gathered to hear him that the shore was packed and there was barely room to move. So Jesus got into a boat and spoke to his followers from the lake. This is the story he told them about the different ways people believe in God.

There was once a farmer who went out to sow his seeds for the next year's harvest. He walked up and down his fields, scattering handfuls of seed to either side. Some seeds fell on the path, where the birds swooped down and quickly gobbled them up. This is like people who hear God's words but don't take any notice of them because they think they know better.

Some seeds fell on rough, stony ground where the seedlings could not take root and soon withered away and died. This is like people who believe in God but only for a short while. When times get tough, they lose their faith.

Some seeds fell among the thistles and thorns which choked the seedlings as they tried to grow. This is like people who love money and possessions so much that it chokes their belief in God.

But some seeds fell in rich, fertile soil where they quickly took root and sprouted, growing tall and strong, and ready to harvest. This is like people who believe in God with all their hearts and minds.

STORYTELLERSTORYTELLERSTORYTELLERSTORYTELLERSTORYTELLERSTORYTELLERSTORYTELLERSTORYTELLERSTORYTELLERSTORYTELLERSTORYTELLERSTORYTELLERSTORYTELLERSTORYTELL

Did you know?

The story of the sower and the seed is called a parable, a story with a special meaning. In them, Jesus used everyday experiences to explain difficult ideas. Many of his audience would have been farmers.

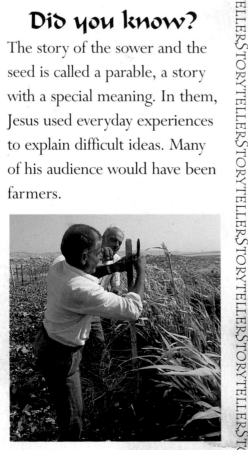

The Lost Sheep

Among the people who came to hear Jesus teach were many who had done wrong in their lives. Jesus welcomed them all and did not turn anyone away. Some people were angry with Jesus for doing this. To show them that everyone matters to God, whatever they have done, Jesus told them the story of the good shepherd.

A shepherd once had a flock of a hundred fine sheep. One night, as he was leading the sheep into their fold, he noticed that one was missing. Even though the shepherd had ninety-nine other sheep to look after, he left them all behind and searched high and low for the one that was lost. When he found the lost sheep, the shepherd was so overjoyed that he went around telling his neighbours and friends so that they could be happy with him.

Did you know?

In this story, Jesus tried to make people understand more about what God is like. He wanted to show that God loves and cares for everyone especially if they are lost or unhappy. In this case, the sheep is lost because it has strayed away from its flock. But people can also feel lost if they have turned away from God. Jesus used this story to show that God is happy when even one lost person turns back to God, just as the shepherd is happy when one lost sheep is found.

The Prodigal Son

A wealthy farmer had two sons. One day, the younger son came to his father and said, "Father, I don't want to be a farmer anymore. I want to start up my own business. Will you give me my share of my inheritance now?"

His father agreed to his request and gave him his share of money and goods. A few days later, the son said goodbye and set off to live in a faraway country. But instead of making something of himself, and using his money wisely, he wasted it on gambling, fine clothes, and expensive food and wine. Soon he had nothing left.

To make matters worse, the country was gripped by a terrible famine. The harvest failed and people went hungry. With all his money gone, the son was forced to sell his belongings and to beg for scraps of food. Then he found work with a local farmer who sent him into the fields to feed the pigs. By this time, the son was so hungry that he even thought of eating the food that he had been given to feed to the pigs.

"What a mess my life is," he said to himself, miserably. "Even my father's servants are better off than I am. I will go

back to my father and beg his forgiveness. I may not be worthy to be called his son anymore, but perhaps I could work as his servant."

So the son set off for home. When he was still some way away, his father saw him and ran down the road to meet him. He threw his arms around his son's neck and kissed him warmly.

"Father," the son said. "I have been foolish and stupid, and do not deserve to be called your son. I have sinned against you and against God."

"Hush, my son, it does not matter now," his father replied. Then he called for a servant to bring his son a clean robe and some new shoes for his feet. "Get ready the finest feast this house has seen. Tonight we will eat like kings and be happy. For I thought that my beloved son was dead but now he has come back home."

Meanwhile, the farmer's elder son was hard at work in the fields. When he heard the sound of music coming from the house, he was surprised and asked one of his men what was going on.

"Your brother has come home," the man told him, "and your father is holding a feast to celebrate his return."

The elder son was furious. How could his father treat his no-good brother like that? He refused to go back into the house or to greet his brother. In the end, his father came out to look for him.

"Whatever is wrong, my son?" the father asked. "Come inside and welcome your brother home."

"But father," the son began, "I have worked so hard for you and never complained or disobeyed your orders. And yet I've never be given anything in return. But my brother who has wasted your money and brought you nothing but shame is welcomed home with a splendid feast! How can that be fair?"

"My son," replied his father, kindly. "You are dearer to me than anyone. Do not worry about that. And everything I have will one day be yours. But today is for being happy and joyful. Your brother was lost and now he is found. Come and join the celebrations."

Did you know?

Jesus told the story of the prodigal, or wasteful, son to teach people about forgiveness. Even though the son has acted badly, his father forgives him at once and treats him like an honoured guest. In the same way, Jesus said, God is like a loving parent who forgives people who have done wrong, whatever they have done and without asking for anything in return.

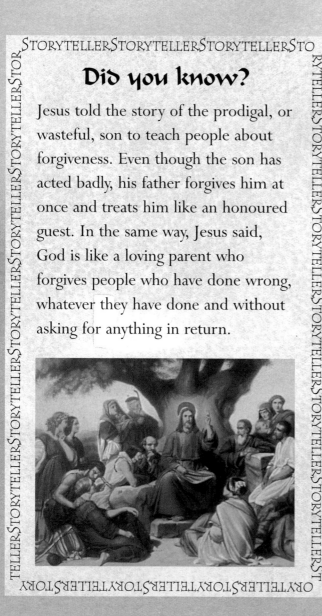

Did you know?

One of the most important Christian prayers is called the Lord's Prayer. It is a prayer which Jesus taught to his disciples. Asking for forgiveness is a key part of the prayer.

Our Father, which art in Heaven
Hallowed be thy name.
Thy kingdom come,
Thy will be done,
In earth as it is in Heaven.
Give us this day our daily bread,
And forgive us our trespasses
As we forgive them that trespass
    against us.
And lead us not into temptation
But deliver us from evil.
For thine is the kingdom,
The power and the glory,
For ever and ever.
            Amen.

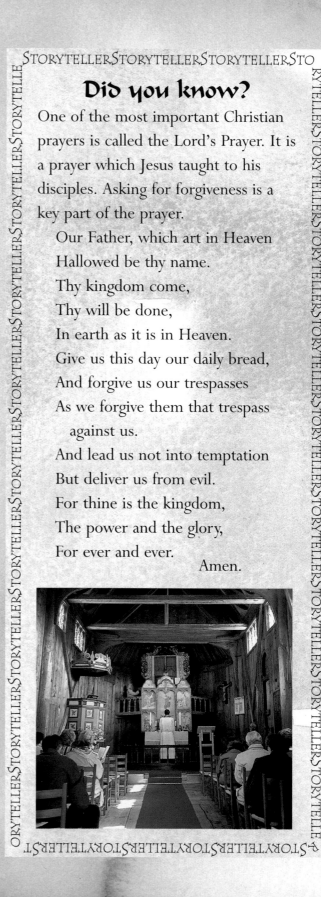

The Story of Easter

At the time of the festival of Passover, Jesus travelled to Jerusalem with his disciples. He knew that his life was in danger for there were many religious priests and leaders in Jerusalem who did not like what he taught and saw him as a threat to them. But the ordinary people flocked to see him. As Jesus rode into the city on a donkey, they lined the streets to greet him. Some spread their coats on the ground in front of him. Others waved long branches of palm leaves. It was a welcome fit for any king.

A few days later, Jesus sat down with his disciples to share a special Passover feast. It should have been a happy occasion but Jesus seemed tired and sad.

"This is the last meal we will share together," he told the astonished disciples. Then he picked up some bread, blessed it and broke it into pieces.

"Eat this bread," he said. "This is to remind you of me."

Then he poured a cup of wine and passed it round for them all to share.

"Drink this wine," he said. "This is to remind you that my blood will be shed for you."

The disciples did what Jesus asked and wondered why Jesus had said that this would be their last meal together. What was going to happen? Jesus's next words sent shivers down their spines.

"One of you sitting here will betray me," he said.

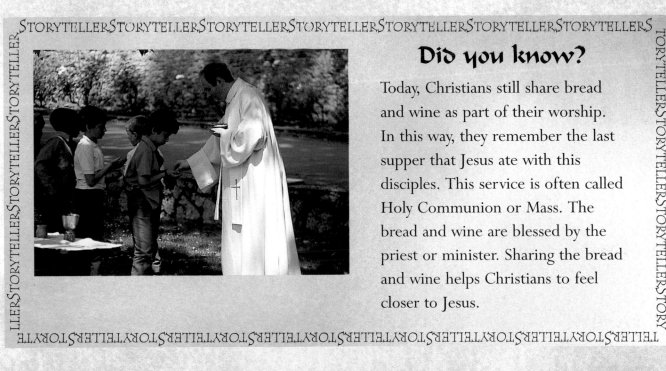

Did you know?

Today, Christians still share bread and wine as part of their worship. In this way, they remember the last supper that Jesus ate with this disciples. This service is often called Holy Communion or Mass. The bread and wine are blessed by the priest or minister. Sharing the bread and wine helps Christians to feel closer to Jesus.

The disciples were stunned. They could not believe their ears. They loved Jesus. Why would any of them want to betray him?

Quietly, Simon Peter asked, "Lord, who will it be?"

Jesus did not reply, but he took a piece of bread and dipped it in some wine. Then he handed it to Judas and said, "Go and do what you have to do." For Jesus's enemies had offered Judas thirty pieces of silver to betray his master. Judas rushed out of the room.

Later that night, Jesus went with the disciples to the Garden of Gethsemane to pray. While they were there, Judas led the soldiers to him.

"The man I kiss is the one you want," Judas whispered to the soldiers. Then he went up to Jesus and kissed him.

At once, the soldiers grabbed Jesus and arrested him. They led him first to the priests who accused him of blasphemy. On the next day, they took him to the Roman governor, Pontius Pilate, who sentenced him to death. Jesus was taken to a place called Golgotha, the Place of the Skull, and nailed to a cross and left to die.

"Forgive them, Father," Jesus prayed through his pain. "For they do not understand what they are doing."

Later that day, Jesus died.

Some of Jesus's friends lifted his body gently down from the cross and wrapped it in a white robe. Then they placed it in a tomb cut out of the rock. With heavy hearts, they rolled a stone across the entrance and wept. They thought that they would never see Jesus again.

Three days later, they returned to the tomb and an amazing sight. The stone had been rolled away and the tomb was empty. Jesus's body had gone! Now an angel, dressed in brilliant white, stood beside the tomb. Before anyone could find their voice, the angel spoke:

"Don't be afraid," the angel said. "I know that you are looking for Jesus. But he is not here. For he has risen from the dead and has come back to life."

Jesus's friends were filled with hope and joy. But they were also worried. The news seemed too good to be true. How could Jesus have come back to life after they had seen him die? But as they ran to tell the others what they had heard, a man came to meet them. They didn't recognise him but when they heard him speak, they knew that the angel had been telling the truth. For the man was Jesus!

Did you know?

The cross is very important for Christians. It reminds them of Jesus's death and Resurrection. A crucifix is a cross with a figure on it to show how Jesus died. A plain cross does not have a figure. It shows that Jesus has risen from the dead. It sometimes has five jewels on it to show the five wounds that Jesus suffered when he was nailed to the cross.

STORYTELLERStorytellerStorytellers

Did you know?

Every year, at Easter, Christians remember Jesus's death. Jesus died on a Friday. This is called Good Friday. This is a sad and sombre time. He rose from the dead on Easter Sunday. This is a very happy day for Christians when they give thanks to God for Jesus's life. Christians believe that Jesus died to make the world a better place and to give people hope for a future with God. Jesus rose from the dead and is with God forever. This is called the Resurrection.

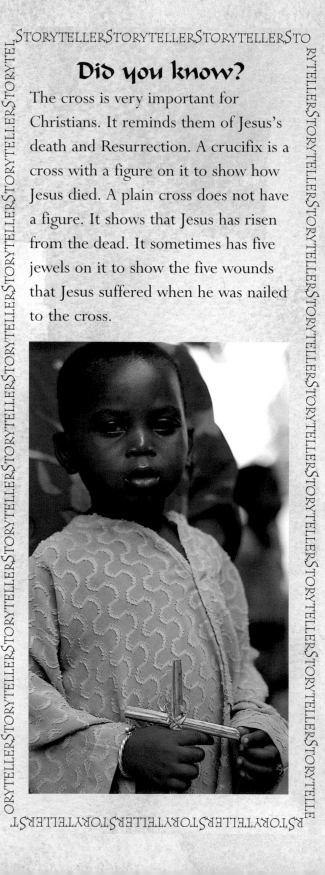

Glossary

Baptism A ceremony at which a person becomes a full member of the Christian Church. Also called Christening.

Bethlehem A town in Palestine where Jesus was born.

Bible The holy scriptures of the Christians.

Blasphemy Words or deeds that insult God.

Christening Another name for Baptism.

Christianity The religion of the Christians. They follow the teachings of Jesus.

Christmas The festival when Christians remember Jesus's birth. It is usually celebrated on 25 December.

Disciple One of Jesus's followers.

Frankincense A sticky gum from a tree which gives off a sweet smell when it is burned.

Gabriel The angel who brought news of Jesus's birth.

Gospels The first four books of the New Testament. They tell of Jesus's life and teachings. They were written by four early Christians, Matthew, Mark, Luke and John.

Herod The king of Jerusalem in Jesus's time.

Holy Spirit The mysterious power of God. It is often shown as a flame, a gust of wind or a white dove.

Jerusalem The city in Palestine where Jesus spent his last days and was crucified on the cross. It was the capital of Palestine.

Jesus A man who lived in Palestine about 2000 years ago. Christians believe that he was the son of God. They follow his teachings as a guide for their lives.

Jews People who follow the religion of Judaism. It began in the Middle East more than 4000 years ago. The people who lived in Palestine in Jesus's time were mostly Jews.

John the Baptist The cousin of Jesus who preached to people and baptised them in the River Jordan to wash away their sins. Jesus asked John to baptise him.

Joseph Jesus's earthly father. He was a carpenter from Nazareth.

Judas The disciple who betrayed Jesus.

Last Supper The last meal Jesus ate with his disciples before his death.

Lord's Prayer A prayer that Jesus taught to his disciples. It is a very special prayer for Christians today.

Mary Jesus's mother. Christians believe that she was specially chosen by God.

Myrrh A sticky gum from certain plants which gives off a sweet smell when it is burned. It is also used in perfumes.

Nazareth A town in Palestine where Jesus lived with his family.

New Testament Part of the Christian Bible. It tells of Jesus's life and of the early Christians.

Palestine The country in the Middle East where Jesus lived and taught. Today, much of Palestine is called Israel.

Parable A story with a special meaning. Jesus often used parables in his teaching.

Passover A Jewish festival which is held in March or April. It is celebrated with a special meal.

Pontius Pilate In Jesus's time, Palestine was ruled by the Romans. Pontius Pilate was the Roman governor. He ruled on behalf of the Roman emperor.

Prodigal Wasteful.

Samaritan A person from the city of Samaria in Palestine. In Jesus's time, the Jews and the Samaritans did not get along.

Index